Side by Side

Side by Side

20 Collaborative Projects for Crafting with Your Kids

Tsia Carson

Photographs by **Meredith Heuer**

ROOST BOOKS

Boston & London 2012

Roost Books
An imprint of Shambhala Publications, Inc.
Horticultural Hall
300 Massachusetts Avenue
Boston, Massachusetts 02115
roostbooks.com

9 8 7 6 5 4 3 2 1

First Edition
Printed in Thailand

⊗ This edition is printed on acid-free paper that meets the American
National Standards Institute Z39.48 Standard.
♻ Shambhala Publications makes every effort to print on recycled paper.
For more information please visit www.shambhala.com.

Distributed in the United States by Random House, Inc.,
and in Canada by Random House of Canada Ltd

Designed by Flat

Library of Congress Cataloging-in-Publication Data
Carson, Tsia.
Side by side: 20 collaborative projects for crafting with your kids /
Tsia Carson; photographs by Meredith Heuer.—1st ed.
p.   cm.
Includes bibliographical references and index.
ISBN 978-1-59030-956-8 (pbk.: alk. paper)
1. Handicraft. I. Title.
TT157.C284 2012
745.5—dc23
2011043089

For my beautiful, crafty daughter

Contents

PART THREE

Family Field Trips

Introduction

A good day is when my daughter, Cedar, and I can spend an afternoon immersed in the activity of making stuff. I might be knitting while she works on an intricate bracelet with pipe cleaners and glow-in-the-dark beads. Or, I might be crocheting in the round while she practices chain stitching.

These moments are some of the happiest we have: simply sitting on the couch, side by side, not talking much, and helping each other with the work—both with encouragement and technique. Just being together.

The crafts in this book center on this ideal—working side by side with your child and enjoying each other's company. At the end of an afternoon, you may emerge with something beautiful to cherish, or you may simply have pleasant memories of making stuff. Either way, the projects that follow can help get you to that magical place where you and your kids are happy and engrossed in the now.

Most child-parent craft projects I have encountered fall into two categories: either you must do everything together, and if your child gets distracted, the project fails; or else you set up an activity for your child to do so you can walk away and do something else, something more "important." This book advocates a third way.

Crafting is an opportunity for me to slow down and spend time with my daughter. I know that, for some parents, this ability to slow down comes more naturally. In my life, I struggle to ignore the various calls of duty: work, straightening up, making dinner, or running errands. I am always rushing my daughter. Somehow, I find the quiet purposefulness of crafting as a way to escape that pressure.

Crafting with my daughter allows me to see how she thinks, how she approaches a problem in her own way, often in a way I never would have considered. In turn, she gets to see how my mind works. This sharing offers a very intimate glimpse into another person.

Crafting also allows me to shower my daughter with compliments. Sometimes being a child is so hard, I'm always looking for a way to praise her. Besides, everything she makes is so beautiful!

Good parenting means providing love, food, and shelter—craft is a major way I manifest my love for Cedar. Many projects in this book are inspired by my desire to surprise her with new ideas. What if we made a paper snowflake as big as our living room? What if we made a playhouse out of living trees? What if I crocheted something that looked just like seaweed? What if I took your favorite old T-shirt and made a pillowcase? What if we took all these pom-poms and made flowers out of them? What if . . . what if. . . ? This game of "what if" expands my daughter's ideas of what is possible. This imagining opens up a future to her, one in which she creates her own answers to life's problems.

One of the best things these projects have taught my daughter is how to turn basic materials into something greater than their sum. In other words, what I am really trying to show her is how the creative process is in its essence alchemical. I want Cedar to understand that what she creates becomes more valuable because of the energy and thought she puts into it. She can transform the simplest materials into gold.

I am a child of the seventies, and as such, I had a great childhood of making things. It was a golden era of free-form plaster casting in the sandbox, creating stuffed-paper sculptures of our spirit animals, and crocheting endlessly with rainbow-colored, self-striping acrylic yarn. I grew up surrounded by craftiness and its pleasant memories of excitement and purpose. I'm trying to give this gift to my daughter so she can share it throughout her life.

How to Use This Book

Working side by side with your child can take many different forms, and so the projects in this book also take different forms and approaches. Here, you'll find twenty projects organized into three main sections: Part One: Collaborators presents projects that let you work together on the craft. In some, you tackle the projects with your kids as a partner, and in some, you serve as a helper, only entering when your child really needs something of you. Part Two: Companions has projects where you work in parallel on similar crafts. For these projects, two related crafts are presented—one at your level and one at your children's level. Your projects are more focused on a final, finished product, while the ones geared to your children are more process-oriented. Part Three: Family Field Trips offers projects that let you explore the outside world together. These projects allow your family to more actively participate in making stuff together in new settings. In the back of the book, techniques and material resources are included to help you create the projects.

Think of this book as a jumping-off point for side-by-side crafting with your family. Treat these crafts as experiments, and work in any way that suits you and your child. You will quickly discover which projects resonate with your kids. By providing simple frameworks, these projects help you and your kids improvise your own solutions. Prepare yourself for surprises!

Tips for Crafting with Kids

I find working with kids to be very natural, especially when I know them well. If I start working on something, a child will almost certainly gravitate toward me to see what I am doing and get involved. But, for parents not as immersed in making stuff, I want to share my set of secrets to help them understand how to craft with kids.

Be Into It
Work on something that interests you and your kids. Be excited about it. Otherwise, the child won't engage. Make yourself very present. Remember: You light the path.

Set the Stage
You're not just working on a craft project; you're embarking on a journey together. Upsell it. Make it extraordinary. Setting the stage builds excitement.

Think Big
You can transform any project into a big event. Basically, any good, standard project made on a gigantic scale, in public, or from unusual materials changes it from a humdrum activity to a dramatic event. Explore with scale, location, and materials.

Stack the Deck
Kids' crafts inevitably conjure up images of puffy paint T-shirts, foam shamrocks stuck to plastic cups, and whatever out-of-the-box stuff you find at a craft chain store. In other words, kids' crafts are associated with things you don't really need or want. They are ugly and go into the garbage when no one is looking. They simply reflect how disposable our culture is: just as there is junk food, there is junk craft. Junk culture is not a natural or inevitable outcome in our lives. It is a choice that we make every day based on our pocketbooks, our need for convenience, and our misconception of what is normal. However, you don't have to make ugly stuff or have your kids make ugly stuff.

I believe that children's crafts are an opportunity to develop discernment and ingenuity. Using generally sustainable, naturally based, and well-made materials helps communicate consideration and respect, which I feel translates into a respect for other parts of your children's lives, including human interactions and the natural world.

In short, feel free to stack the deck. You can use high-quality materials and edit the supplies to focus the palette and textures of the project.

Keep It Simple

More choices are not better for kids when it comes to making crafts. Neither are complex workflows. That is why this book focuses on very simple activities with room to explore variations. Mastery is deeply satisfying for child and adult alike. Let that joy happen! Start simple, and build at your child's pace to create more complex end products.

Lose Expectations

Once you have assembled the basic materials, focus on the process, not the vision of the end product. You might have a very definitive end product in mind, but that vision almost always results in tears (yours) because children will do what they want. If the project doesn't turn out how you expected, so what? Remember: It's about the doing.
Or perhaps you might seek to make a project educational—whether you think this afternoon will somehow get them into college or you want to teach them something. Any pressure you exert here will just make the project a chore, and that approach defeats the purpose. Instead, choose to embrace the unexpected.

Let the Child Lead

If you haven't already figured it out, your child is smarter than you. Children bring a fresh perspective to an experience and can see things that you, set in your habitual ways, will overlook. If you let your child lead, you will learn things about the project, about creativity, and about your kid that you would never otherwise discover. When Cedar was working on snowflakes with me, I had very definite ideas about the right way to cut a snowflake: make a quadruple fold from a square piece of paper, cut the paper round, and so on. She showed me how to fold the paper vertically and get a beautiful snowflake. Who knew? I have often found that when she is directing and I can help be her hands, what we are doing ends up being much more interesting.

Avoid Comparisons

It's important when working side by side to avoid trying to do matching projects. Inevitably, an adult, with greater fine motor skills and better hand-eye coordination, will make a more polished end result. For example, if you and your child are both working on a sewn doll, there is a good chance that your child will feel bad about her doll when she compares it to the one you are making. The less you invite comparison, the better. Create side-by-side activities where a technique is shared, but make the projects themselves different.

Make a Mess

I cannot tell a lie. Any of the projects in this book will make a mess. I'm sorry; being messy is just part of the creative process. Here's what you do to deal with this onslaught: designate an area of the house where the project will happen, and then properly protect the floor and furniture in that area. Then you won't have a conniption when something gets spilled or when things get sticky.

Getting Started

Here is a list of items that are good things to have on hand to encourage creativity and crafting in your home. Project-specific materials are listed at the start of each project.

Basics

Cutting implements (scissors, pinking shears, rotary cutters, paper slicers—use sense when sharing with children)

Pads of drawing paper (basically, any size and type)

Pens (markers, ballpoints)

Pencils (colored, no. 2)

Pencil sharpener (an electric sharpener—a whole afternoon of fun, in and of itself)

Paints (water, poster)

Glue (white, clear, stick, glitter)

Tape (masking, scotch—kids love all tapes)

Crochet hooks and knitting needles (assorted, and perhaps a knitting nancy for making I-cord, too)

String (kitchen, hemp)

Sewing supplies (many sizes of needles, basic cotton thread, straight pins, a seam ripper)

Things to Save

Yarn (all weights and fuzziness)

Notions (ribbons and trims)

Buttons, beads, and feathers

Threads (sewing, floss, sparkly, in many colors)

Colorful paper (origami, wrapping, greeting cards)

Fabric (cotton, linen, old sweaters and T-shirts, burlap, scrap)

Natural objects (pine cones, seed pods, sea glass)

Nice to Have

Sewing machine (in good working order)

Glue gun

Iron (always comes in handy for finishing stuff up)

PART ONE

Collaborators

These projects work with larger groups of kids.

The projects in this section are all about collaborating with your child. Accomplishing these projects together, you can get your hands dirty and share the joy of the journey toward a common goal.

Sometimes, you will both work on the very same element of the project, and other times, you will be taking turns. You may only be involved in one aspect of a project, or you may be involved in all areas. No matter what tasks you each perform during each project, you are always working side by side.

Collaborating on projects with kids is very different from collaborating with adults. Remember that what is fair for two adults is very different from what is fair between a child and an adult. When you are working with kids, splitting tasks fifty-fifty is just not fair. With their (sometimes) shorter attention spans, fine motor skills that are still developing, and a lack of maturity that would let them delay gratification, children's frustrations can surface more quickly. Therefore, true collaboration with children means letting them take control of the project so they have a voice. This approach will engage them with the project, and it will reduce frustration levels significantly.

Collaborating with children may also require that you be their hands, that you are primarily responsible for set up and clean up, and that you do a lot of the menial tasks that drag a project down, from a child's perspective. However, I never find doing this part of the work tiresome. Instead, I find that watching kids as they come up with a unique, creative solution is just as interesting and active as making the project itself.

Your role here is primarily to provide suggestions and to help the project start; where it goes is best left up to the child. Think of your job as opening a door—watch your kids run ahead, and try to catch up. It's wonderful!

Giant Newspaper Snowflake

Sure, you already know how to make a paper snowflake. But when you change the scale from small to gigantic, something magical happens.

The humble paper snowflake, a beloved, simple craft, becomes heroic. It draws everyone in and turns an intimate, singular activity into a chatty, fun group play date. Kids and adults work together in this activity to fold and cut.

Since these giant snowflakes take longer to fold and cut than their smaller cousins, the grand reveal becomes an event. Anticipation and hand clapping ensue. The giant snowflake revealed becomes a playground for kids to jump over and color—and kids become inspired to cut some more.

Project Notes

Prepare a few giant pieces of newspaper so you can enjoy this activity several times. Do your best to create a 12-foot or larger square of taped-together newspaper for each giant snowflake you wish to create.

Paper snowflakes work no matter how you cut the paper. However, we have included snowflake templates (see technical notes) if you want to impress your kids with some fancy cutwork. Remember that the more the paper is folded, the more complex the cutting will appear when unfolded, and that cutting away more paper yields a better result.

While working with your child on this project, be prepared to join in with your scissors to help make some of the deeper cuts. Children who are used to working on a small scale may not be prepared to cut out the very large pieces of paper that give the snowflake its interesting shape.

This project seems like such a simple one, and yet it has infinite variations. Indestructible Tyvek would beat newsprint for durability in the giant snowflake. If made from tissue paper, snowflakes can be sewn together into flower forms; these will float nicely when tossed from the top of the stairs.

Once you make the giant snowflakes, kids won't want to stop the snowflake cutting, so be sure to have some smaller paper handy for the kids to keep creating. At our house, we have a fondness for origami paper, which comes in a perfect size and weight to cut smaller-scale snowflakes.

Materials

A newspaper

Scissors

Masking tape

String

Chalk

Other paper to cut

Create a giant square piece of newsprint by using masking tape to attach the newspaper pages edge to edge. This giant square should be at least 12 feet per side to account for the area lost when you round the paper.

Create a quadruple fold. To do this step, fold the paper in half, corner to corner, to form a triangle. Continue folding the paper on the diagonal to create increasingly thinner triangles.

Round off the snowflake. Take a piece of string, and tie a piece of chalk to the end. Hold or tape down the end of the string to the folded paper's triangle tip, and extend the chalk to the top of the paper. Draw a curved line with the chalk along the top of the triangle. To draw the line, make sure the string is

"Doing them with tissue paper is the best. They're perfect for tossing down the stairs."

—Cedar

pulled taut as it extends from side to side across the triangle. Cut along the chalk line to create the curve necessary for a circular snowflake.

Cut into that triangle with a pair of sharp scissors. Be sure not to cut all the way across the triangle! The more cuts you make and the more surface area that you remove, the more intricate your snowflake will look.

Reveal your giant snowflake by carefully unfolding the paper.

Pom-Pom Garland

The pom-pom is a glorious thing: it's small, round, and fluffy. Pom-poms are also fun and satisfying to make—the youngest kid can make these perfect spheres of yarn and get a profound sense of accomplishment.

Making pom-poms is fun, but what can you do with them? This project reimagines the pom-pom as a fluffy flower to make a decorative garland, which becomes a cheerful reminder of the all that pom-pom-making joy.

Children can be equal partners in all aspects of this project, from making the pom-pom flowers to cutting the felt leaves and crocheting or braiding the vine. All parts of the activity can also be passed seamlessly back and forth between adult and child. It is perfect in its simplicity.

What I loved the most about this project was that it was easy to do over several afternoons without losing momentum. My daughter instantly got the vision, and the final sewing together of the pieces provided me with an adult version of the sense of satisfaction that Cedar felt making the perfect pom-poms.

Not only are the pieces of this project fun to make, but the finished garland is a homemade way to dress up a party or decorate your child's room.

Project Notes

The length of the vine can be determined by where you plan to hang or drape your garland.

The number of pom-pom flowers is a personal preference, but I find that more is always better. You can use any excess pom-poms in another project.

I advocate for a pom-pom maker, which I would have said was a ridiculous accoutrement until I invested in one. If you don't have a pom-pom maker, see the technical notes for how to make a pom-pom without one.

Pom-poms are yarn intensive, so you will want to use inexpensive yarn. This project is a great place to emphasize the palette, harmonizing the colors of the pom-pom flowers in a way that pleases you. A good place to start is to pick the pom-pom colors from within a color family: pinks and reds, or adjacent colors on a color wheel, purples and blues.

This activity has no hard order or step sequence. In the end, you will need a long piece of green vine to which you will attach your pom-pom flowers and felt leaves.

Materials

Yarn (various weights and colors)

Scissors

Crochet hook

Needle and thread

Felt squares (various greens)

Pom-pom maker (optional)

"I enjoyed cutting the string for the pom-poms. I could do it all day. It's hard to explain why."

—Cedar

Create the vine. Using a very chunky yarn, crochet the vine using a chain stitch (see technical notes for Precious Keepsakes project) or braid it. A crocheted vine is a wonderful starting crochet project for a child, since there is no pressure to create even stitches. A braided vine may be an easier way for younger children to help.

Create the pom-pom flowers. Using a pom-pom maker or following the instructions in the technical notes, make several sizes of pom-poms so that you can make clusters of flowers on the vine.

Create the leaves. Cut leaf shapes out of the felt. We layered three sheets of craft felt in different shades of green and cut them together so that each flower cluster got three different-colored leaves of approximately the same shape. Taking turns, we freehand cut the felt layers in rough ovoid shapes.

Attach the flowers to the vine. Lay out all your pom-poms and your vine. Place the flowers in clusters fairly evenly along the vine, paying attention to how you distribute color across it. Fan the leaves out and secure them to vine with a needle and thread, alternating their position (left/right, top/bottom). Sew the flower clusters on top of leaves to cover the stitches.

Hang it up!

Potato Print Milky Way

Potato prints are an old standby of children's craft projects, perhaps because they are easy to do and use readily available materials.

This approach to potato prints focuses the project on an astronomical theme, which reduces the variety of shapes, colors, and mediums used. The star-shaped stamps and light-colored paints allow kids the freedom to explore composition, rather than materials. These restrictions are also key to the project's success in maintaining children's interest. When they are engaged, they are better able to make meaningful, aesthetic choices and create a coherent finished product. While end products are not the main focus of projects in this book, in this case, the finished project does provide a nice sense of accomplishment for the child.

Despite the project's simplicity, preparation and set up are involved, so you may want to create the potato stamps the night before you introduce this craft to your child. Once the stamping begins, this project is an excellent chance to work on your facilitation skills, to be a technical resource—in other words, to be an inker of potatoes!

I find doing this project in the kitchen is a great Saturday morning activity for a few kids with a lot of pent-up stamping energy. And, perhaps, if you can keep the materials out for the day, you'll be able to squeeze in your own adult potato print project when you find a quiet moment!

Project Notes

Star cookie cutters are readily available in craft and cooking stores, as well as online (see resources). If you're working with one child, you might be able to do your own potato print project at the same time. With two to four children, you will need to assume the role of stamp cleaner and inker.

You can prepare the potato stamps the night before. Simply refrigerate the finished potatoes, either wrapped tightly in plastic or with the stamp area facedown in a shallow plate of water.

Clean the potatoes, and cut them lengthwise to produce the biggest possible area with which to stamp.

Create the star stamp by pressing the star cookie cutter into the potato and using a knife to cut away the potato outside of the cookie cutter. Carefully remove the cookie cutter to reveal the star stamp.

Set up your work area. Spread newspaper or kraft paper over your work table. Create a cardboard cutout to fit inside the T-shirt by tracing the T-shirt on cardboard and cutting it out. Place the cardboard cutout inside the shirt so the ink doesn't bleed through to the back of the shirt.

Prep your materials. Fill a shallow bowl with water to rinse the potatoes. Squeeze the fabric paints onto a tray, and spread them out with the spatula or ink roller.

Materials

6–8 potatoes

Small star cookie cutters

Knife

Fabric paint (in assorted yellow and gold colors)

Cardboard

Newspaper or brown kraft paper

Tray

Shallow bowl

Silicon spatula or ink roller

Dark T-shirts and/or bandanas

Stamp your shirt. Dip the potato stamp into the fabric paint, and then stamp your shirt. Use a different potato star for each color, or wash off the potatoes in between stamps to keep the colors true. If you like, show your child images of the Milky Way or constellations as inspiration—and then let them stamp away!

Set the fabric paint by following the manufacturer's instructions (this usually means ironing).

Glitter Glue Monoprint

Here's a well-known fact: children love to take a tube of glitter glue and squeeze a giant pile of it onto a piece of paper while their parents say, "No, no! That's too much!"

Instead of getting uptight when your kid gets expressive with glitter, use it to make beautiful Rorschach-esque monoprints by pressing the papers together. The magic of pulling apart the papers to reveal the final prints works on adult and child alike.

For this project, you will need to help younger children, who will have trouble aligning the papers on top of each other and peeling apart the prints. You can also facilitate an interruption-free creative process by laying things out to dry, making small visual recommendations, and being an expansive force rather than a repressive presence. This change in perspective is the adult reward for this project—it brings you and the kids closer together.

This project is ideal for a play date because each child gets a copy of all the prints. And, who knows? Maybe all the unrestrained squeezing of glitter glue will sublimate the desire to uncontrollably squeeze toothpaste and sunscreen.

Project Notes

Adults should definitely spend time protecting tables, chairs, and floors before setting out this craft.

The secret to this project is to provide a limited amount of paint. Use very small tubes of glitter glue because the urge to squeeze is irresistible! You can replenish them when necessary. Providing limited paint also prevents your child from making a layer of medium so thick that the paper tears.

For older kids, substitute acrylic paint for the glitter glue. Add a drop of dishwashing liquid to the paint so it doesn't dry out before the prints are created.

Prepare your work area with newspaper or kraft paper to protect surfaces. Also, create an area where prints can be set to dry. Pile up the paper you want to use. Set up the paints and/or glitter glue.

Set up your print by laying down the first piece of paper and squeezing a thick layer of glitter glue or other medium onto it.

Make your print by laying another piece of paper on top and smoothing it down. Peel up the top paper to reveal a reflective print. Repeat this step until there is not enough medium on the original paper to create another print.

Lay your prints flat to dry.
This simple project makes you listen to the better angels of your nature to create small, precious things.

Materials

Lots of paper (of the same size). For younger children, a more absorbent paper or construction paper is preferable.

Newspaper or brown kraft paper

Glitter glue or acrylic paint

Small squeeze tubes (optional but suggested)

"The best part is that you get two copies of the same thing. It feels like magic."

—Cedar

Hand-Stamped Bookmarks and Stationery

This is a little project with a big heart! It is a great example of how materials can elevate a mundane craft into something fabulous.

The choice of materials for this project may feel a little over the top, but I always advocate for working with good, high-quality materials with children. This approach teaches respect for materials and places value on what they are making. I also avoid working with very predetermined component parts—such as branded characters or illustrated stickers—as this takes away from learning about composition and distracts from the materiality of the final object.

Using high-quality materials and working at a very small scale helps your children understand the preciousness of what they are using. They can see how very simple materials, like tags and envelopes, can be transformed through the creative process into very valuable things. For an adult, such a small, ephemeral project enables experimentation so that there is no pressure to make a "perfect" bookmark or card. In this way, this project is an engrossing one for adult and child alike. Working alongside your child, being no better or worse, creates a very relaxed atmosphere.

When Cedar and I made these bookmarks, we used hand-carved wood blocks. Using such a rare tool allowed me to explain that people have used these types of wood blocks to make patterned fabrics for many hundreds of years, giving Cedar a small glimpse into artisanal practices. If you can, I recommend adding a traditional tool such as these wood blocks to your making.

I've found that we don't talk much when we do this project. We just show each other moments of what we are working on and share techniques that way.

Project Notes

It may take some foresight to pull together the items for this project, but these materials can be put together over and over again to make this a repeated activity.

I find the bookmarks themselves to be the most useful result of this project as I tend to need indicators in books for repeatedly referenced items like my favorite pancake recipe, knitting abbreviations, and medicine-dosage guidelines for children. In my daughter's case, we are usually reading a few chapter books simultaneously, and it helps not to lose her place.

Materials

Assorted media to print on: craft gift cards, brown kraft paper, envelopes, and hang tags

Indian wood block stamps (used for fabric) or rubber stamps

Washi tape (Japanese decorative masking tape)

Decorative hole punches

Gouache paints

Brushes

Paint palette

Scissors

There is no hard order to the creative steps here. Set a goal. Think about what you want to make so you have a series of options to discuss with your children. Bookmarks are a great starting point, but you could also make thank you cards, small gift cards for upcoming children's parties, or stationery.

Acquire the materials. This project is all about the materials, so pull together an array of media and tools. While I selected some of the stamps, whole punches, and tape for this project, my daughter and I together selected the print media we wanted to use. Involving children in the selection of materials is a good way to engage them in the craft.

Make your bookmarks, cards, or stationery. Once you've selected your materials, start decorating your bookmarks, cards, paper, or envelopes. For adults in particular, this project offers a great way to lose creative inhibitions. Although the materials are special, don't be concerned about wasting them or doing something wrong. Lucky for you, children will not have this problem.

"The choices were so nice, I liked putting the string on the bookmarks."

—*Cedar*

Child-Drawn Stuffed Monster

By Diane Bromberg

My friend Diane gave my daughter a handmade stuffed monster for her birthday. While Diane's projects are always ingenious and exemplary, I was particularly blown away by this softie.

She told me it all started because her daughter really wanted an Ugly Doll, but she didn't want to buy a toy that was so easy to make—this doll is just like a flat drawing, but softer and with stuffing.

So, Diane had her daughters draw a bunch of monsters. They each drew three or four. They laid all the drawings out on the floor and together selected their best monsters. Diane transferred the drawings onto the fabric, and then they worked together to cut and hand sew them into stuffed toys. The power of this project is bringing a child's drawing to life in another medium.

Project Notes

Felt is an ideal fabric for this project because it doesn't need finished edges, so you can cut out appliqué shapes without being concerned about fraying. Making this doll can be a great first sewing project for a child.

Work with your child to draw the doll. It should be something your child is excited to own, but that isn't too hard to sew. Try to keep the overall shape relatively simple. Color isn't terribly important now, but if you have fabric scraps lying around, maybe you can start with those before drawing, matching the fabric scraps to markers or crayons you already have.

Freehand draw the child's drawing to your fabric using a pen or chalk. Don't worry about being too precise; this is a forgiving project. Cut out the doll, leaving a ½" seam allowance around the entire outline.

Embellish the doll. Decorating may involve appliquéing facial details with fabric scraps, embroidering fingernails, or adding whatever details you're inspired to do. This is your chance to give your doll some character.

Place the doll fabric wrong sides together, and sew around the outline, ½" from the edge, with a machine or by hand, leaving a 3" gap. Turn the doll right side out, and poke stuffing into it with the back of a pencil. Sew up the hole.

Materials

Your child's drawing

Pen or chalk

Scraps of fabric

Stuffing

Sewing machine and/or needle and thread

PART TWO

Companions

These projects are intimate and suitable for just you and a child or two.

The true intention of side-by-side crafting is spending time with your kids and fostering that ineffable feeling of togetherness. Working on the same project with your child certainly has rewards, but sometimes, you'll both want to work on your own individual projects.

If you're a crafty parent, perhaps you have your own projects already in process and you can spend a little time working on them. Of course, when you bring out your project, it's very likely that your child will want to do the same thing! This section embraces those moments. Here are projects perfect for those times when you and your child want to work in the same medium, but on separate projects that are fun for each of you. Adjacency is a great form of intimacy.

The projects in this section come in pairs: a kid-appropriate craft and a more involved adult (or older child) craft. The crafts are paired by materials, so if you're making a succulent wreath, your child can be creating a terrarium. Kids' projects almost always require less time, so children usually will stop and watch you work on your project. Observation is a great teacher. Even when I don't explicitly show my daughter how to do a certain task, the next time we sit together, I suddenly see that she has watched a technique and incorporated it into her repertoire.

While the kids' projects in this section take an afternoon, the adult projects may extend across several evenings to complete.

Drawing with Thread

Embroidery is one of those craft forms with a lot of rules. First, you must learn your stitches, then you have to follow a pattern, and, finally, you might be able to make something representational. But, who says that embroidery has to be a proper affair?

One of the simplest joys is to pierce a fabric with a needle. When Cedar was younger, she could spend hours free-form embroidering with the floss tied to the needle. My work was only slightly more sophisticated because I knew a few simple stitches.

Embroidery is an ideal project to do in tandem. This low-intensity activity lets you and your child talk as you work. The materials are very simple and require little adult intervention. Children can quickly learn stitches by watching you work and, if they feel ready, step into more formal applications.

Leaf Embroidery Child

When you choose a leaf as your embroidery canvas, it puts the emphasis on the process of stitching, rather than the final outcome. This technique is a great way to let go of what you should and shouldn't do.

For this craft, my inspiration was the Arabic tradition of calligraphy on leaves, which I had seen a few years ago. In this art form, calligraphers write in gold leaf on specially treated leaves. In our project, we do not show this sort of intricacy and discipline. Instead, children use their own innate sense of composition to stitch into the leaves.

One of the nicest parts of this project is to hunt for leaves appropriate for stitching. Finding that perfect leaf is a great way to teach children about the importance of material selection. Very little oversight is needed for this project, and that is why it can be companioned nicely with the Child Drawing Embroidery (on page 67).

Project Notes

I planted a few giant umbrella leaf plants in the backyard knowing that, at some point, we would put them to good use. Umbrella, Elephant Ear, and Hosta leaves make wonderful canvases. Fall oak leaves are also great to sew into because they are tough.

If your child picks a green leaf, put it in a vase with water when done. A dry leaf is suitable for framing.

Materials

Embroidery floss

Assorted needles (sharps, tapestry/ball point, and embroidery)

Large leaves (dried or fresh)

Assorted plant matter (Indian strawberries, rose petals, clover, grasses)

Scissors

Gather your materials. Go into the backyard, a park, or any natural area with your child, and find big leaves and other interesting plant life to sew together. Make gentle suggestions about material selection.

Select a needle that is appropriate for your child. Tapestry/ball point needles have a dull tip and are excellent for younger children. Tape the tips of embroidery needles if they feel too sharp. Some children have excellent fine motor skills and can be given a sharp needle without fear.

Thread the needle and tie it up. The final length of thread or floss should be no longer than the length from the child's hand to elbow. This will make it easier to sew without snagging. With a very young child, you can tie the short end around the eye of the needle so the child doesn't pull the floss out from the needle while sewing.

Explain a basic stitch. Show the child how to put the needle through the leaf and how to pull the thread through, too. Other than that, do not correct or teach—this activity is all about discovery.

Stay close by. Your child will need help when the thread tangles or when it's time to tie off the thread and start a new one.

Allow the child to determine when it's done. This activity can go from 20 minutes to 4 hours.

"Embroidery is sewing that you can see."

—Cedar

Child Drawing
Embroidery

Adult

My daughter draws all the time. Every once in a while, she makes a drawing that is so beautiful to me I put it into a special pile.

This project is a great way to make one of those special drawings more permanent. It's great for a child to see a parent putting that much care into something the child has created. It fosters a sense of self worth.

Project Notes

Involve your child by having him or her help choose the drawing you are to embroider.

Use a transfer paper or pencil color that contrasts with your fabric color.

Keep a copy of the drawing on hand to refer to while you sew.

Pearl cotton is thinner than embroidery floss, and you can get more subtlety from your stitching by varying the width: 1 strand of floss = #12 pearl cotton; 2 strands of floss = #8 pearl cotton; and 6 strands of floss = #5 pearl cotton.

Don't feel as if you must use a lot of complicated stitches! A simple back stitch (see technical notes) yields impressive results.

Find a drawing both you and your child like—don't worry if it's not perfect. You might want to make a copy of it so that you don't ruin the original product.

Transfer your drawing to the fabric. Place your fabric face up on a firm surface. If using transfer paper, place it color-side down on the fabric. Place the

Materials

Your child's drawing (as messy or colorful as you like)

Transfer paper (optional)

Pencil

Embroidery hoop (9" or more)

Linen or other fabric to embroider

Embroidery floss or pearl cotton

Darning needle

drawing on top of the transfer paper. Firmly, with a pencil, transfer wheel, or ballpoint pen, copy the lines of the drawing. When you lift the paper, you should have faint outlines of the drawing on your fabric. Alternatively, you can use a sharp pencil to lightly freehand the drawing on your fabric— your stitches will cover it up, and you can wash it away later.

Embroider the drawing. Fit your fabric to your embroidery hoop, and then, using embroidery floss reduced to two strands of thread, back stitch (see technical notes) along the outlines to make your child's drawing come to life.

Indoor Succulent Gardens

One day, I noticed Cedar playing with a dollhouse, and it seemed so dull and lifeless. In a flash, I was inspired to make a terrarium—it was like a living dollhouse!

Terrariums are really easy to make, so I knew Cedar could work on one while I worked alongside her creating a succulent wreath, something I had wanted to do for a long time. With big, messy set ups like these projects require, doing two projects at once is smart, since clean up will be the same. I could help my daughter with the terrarium when she needed it, while I worked on the more technically challenging wreath. She would watch me struggle with the wreath and laugh about my obvious black thumb. We did these projects concurrently over a long, lovely afternoon.

Terrarium Child

Terrariums are a great way to help your kids understand landscape design and caretaking. The miniaturized scale really helps focus on how to develop composition. The instructions are detailed, but the project is really quite easy.

In our terrarium, we used about half a dozen succulents. My daughter chose which plants to use, and I helped a bit with the placement. She did most of the patting down of the dirt to settle the plants, and we both brushed the dirt off the plant leaves and the sides of the terrarium. Do not pack in too many plants; they will grow over time and need some room.

Gather your succulents. If you are using clippings from your own plants, give them a few days before planting them so they scab and roots begin to form. If you decide to order from a nursery or online, then look for plants sold in 1" to 2" pots—anything larger will need more space than your terrarium can provide.

Acquire a terrarium. Succulents need plenty of air circulation to thrive, so you will want use an open container for your terrarium (see resources).

Prepare the planting materials. Try to predetermine the amount of gravel, charcoal, and potting mixture you will need to fill your terrarium. Place each of the planting materials in individual bowls that your kids can lift and pour from easily.

Layer the planting materials in the terrarium. (See the diagram in the technical notes.) Fill the terrarium with the first layer of material: gravel or pebbles, approximately 2" thick to ensure proper drainage in your terrarium. This step is vitally important for succulents that do not like to be soggy.

Materials

10–20 succulent clippings or 5–10 succulent plants in 2" pots (any bigger and you'll crowd your terrarium)

Plastic or waste paper to work on

Terrarium form, such as a goldfish bowl (the container must be open for succulents)

Gravel or pebbles

Activated charcoal

Succulent dirt

Mixing bowls

Spray bottle filled with water

Spoon

Brush

Medicine syringe

Rooting hormone (optional)

Fill the terrarium with your second layer of material: activated charcoal, approximately 1" thick. This layer helps the terrarium to stay fresh and clean by discouraging fungal and other plant diseases. Purchase activated charcoal at any pet store in the aquarium area.

Fill the terrarium with your third layer of material: succulent potting mix, approximately 2" thick. This mix is where the succulents will grow. Add some water to your potting mix so that it holds together and becomes denser. Mix it outside your terrarium so that the potting mix you put in the terrarium is moist and suitable for planting. You may consider creating a mound in the middle or "back" of the terrarium to simulate a landscape. Tamp down the potting mix a bit with the back of a spoon.

Ready your succulents for transplant. If you are using cuttings, remove any leaves that will be below the dirt, leaving approximately ½" stem. Taller specimens may need longer stems to balance. You may also consider using rooting hormone to encourage the plants to root (follow the manufacturer's directions). If you are using store-bought plants, you will want to take them out of their pots to make sure that their roots are wet (which makes them more pliable). You can spray the dirt and roots with a spray bottle of lukewarm water to moisten them. Gently aerate the roots by making pencil-sized holes throughout the dirt around them. Most plants will be root-bound, meaning that the roots have grown around and around inside the pot. These roots can be gently broken up to encourage the plants to grow new, healthier root systems.

Place your succulents in the terrarium. This part is tricky. Pretend that you are creating a forest. Gently guide your child's selection by placing the tallest specimens in the middle or back of the terrarium, the medium-sized ones in the mound or in front, and your ground-hugging variety along the edges where they can be seen. The point is to make all the succulents visible and give them their own room to shine.

Plant the succulents. By looking at the size of the plant's roots, you can figure out how big to make the hole. Make sure that the dirt around the plant is patted down to ensure good contact between the specimen and the potting mix. Use the medicine syringe to water precisely around your plant—not too much, though!

Take care of your terrarium. Keep your terrarium out of very intense, direct sun because the glass magnifies and heats the sunlight, which can burn the plants. Do not allow the leaves to touch the terrarium glass, which will cause rot and fungal disease. Remove any dead or diseased plants or leaves from the terrarium immediately. Because of the semi-enclosed environment, disease will pass through the plants quickly. Prune your plants so they stay the size you want. If a plant grows in an ungainly fashion, simply remove it.

Wreath Adult

Succulent wreaths are a welcome sign of life during the late winter. I had seen these wreaths and was itching for an excuse to make one. My daughter's terrarium project was the perfect opportunity.

Although we had created terrariums before, the wreath was a first, so Cedar was very interested in the whole process. This type of creative manipulation of plants seems to open a child's mind about what one can do with gardening. And my trial-and-error approach really helped my daughter see that we were at the same level—excited novices. It's great to let kids in on the fact that you are always learning, too. This is a big, messy project, so be prepared.

Materials

20 succulent clippings or 5–10 succulent plants in 2" pots

Plastic or waste paper to work on

Sphagnum moss

Wreath form

Florist wire

Bucket

Pencil

Create the wreath form. Fill a bucket with water, and immerse the sphagnum moss in it for 15 to 30 minutes. Take your wreath form, and fill the bottom and the sides with wet sphagnum moss, brown side down. This step will prevent dirt from leaking out the bottom. Create a pre-moistened layer of potting mix on top of the sphagnum moss. Take more wet sphagnum moss, and place it on the top and sides so that moss completely covers the potting mix. Wrap the entire thing—frame, moss, and soil—in floral wire. Don't make the floral wire too tight, or you will need to push it around to place your plants. This wreath form can be made ahead of time and soaked prior to use.

Place your succulents. Again, this part is the tricky business. Some people, more methodical than I, would begin by digging small holes and planting their succulents in layers that face the same direction. After each layer, they would wrap additional wire to hold the specimens in place, being careful the floral wire does not cut into the succulents; they would arrange the next layer of succulents to hide how the first layer was attached. They would ring around the wreath until they came back to the beginning, and then would hide their wrapping with a final layer of succulents.

That is not what I did at all. Instead, I selected three of each type of succulent I liked, focusing on the rosette forms because they felt floral, and I placed them in rough triangles around the wreath. This method created a fairly balanced composition. We kept adding more specimens, in a somewhat even fashion, trying to vary color and texture until we got tired. Then I wrapped the whole thing in florist wire to hold it together.

Find a method for placing the plants that works for you. No matter how you go about this task, be sure to firmly place each succulent into the potting mix sandwiched in the wreath form and to secure each plant with floral wire.

Take care of your wreath. Let the wreath lie flat for the next 3 to 6 months so the plants firmly root into the soil. If storing the wreath indoors, it will need a platter or plastic sheeting underneath it. The wreath requires very little care: a dunk in a sink of lukewarm water every week or so for 15 minutes should give it the moisture it needs. Keep your wreath out of direct sun for the first few days, so it doesn't go into shock.

Hang your wreath. After 3 to 6 months, the roots of the plants are fully developed, and the wreath can be hung just as you would any nonliving wreath.

Handmade Pillows

My daughter doesn't like stuffed animals, but she won't go to sleep without her special little pillow. One night, I realized I had no clean case for her pillow. I found an old T-shirt of hers and popped it on the pillow—a perfect fit! I thought, "What a great pillowcase."

And so I made her a couple from beloved T-shirts that didn't fit her anymore. Watching me, my daughter got inspired. So, we worked on a simple running stitch so she could make pillows, too. Teaching a simple stitch—and not being too bossy about it all—can lead to hours of careful work. She cut her own fabric to create a pillow. What I love the most about it is its funny shape. The point with this project is that creativity is contagious. If you have an epiphany, your child will see that and want to share your inspiration and make something, too. Instead of waiting to do this work until later, create a tandem project that invites your child into the excitement.

Running-Stitch Pillow Child

This pillow took my daughter several sessions to complete. She chose the fabric from a pile of large scraps I had and cut the shape. She only needed me to thread her needle.

Several times, I had to help untangle her stitches, sometimes losing a few while I tied the thread off. But she got progressively better at sewing, so that by the time she sewed the third side, she made no mistakes at all.

Project Notes

Felt and cotton jersey are great choices for this project, since their edges won't fray.

Stuff the stuffing in using a pencil.

Fold the fabric in half, or layer two pieces, wrong sides together. Cut out whatever shape you like through both layers.

Thread the needle. This step is where the adult comes in. It may be helpful to tie the thread to the eye of the needle so that it can't slip through. Knot the end of the thread.

Stitch your pillow together. Keep the fabric wrong sides together, and sew together using a running stitch (see technical notes) along the outer edge of the fabric, leaving ½–¾" of material so the stitch stays secure. To make a more professional-looking pillow, layer the fabric right sides together, sew along the edges (leaving a small gap), and then turn the pillow inside out so the seams are on the inside.

Finish your pillow. When you have sewn all but a few inches of the pillow, stuff it and then sew up the hole.

Materials

Fabric

Needle and thread

Scissors

Pencil

Stuffing

T-shirt Pillow Case Adult

This is an aha! project. I am always looking for ways to recycle my daughter's clothes.

It was so rewarding to do this transformative thing to one of her old T-shirts and get her ideas about which T-shirts to use and how to put them together. Her face lit up when I put a new case on her pillow—that is when she really got the project. Plus, it is easy peasy to sew, so you can keep up a good conversation as you both work.

Project Notes

Sewing skill is not a big part of this project. I only recommend using a machine to sew this pillow case so that it can be thrown into the wash without worry. If you have a serger to use, that's awesome. Consult your sewing machine manual for how to stitch cotton jersey.

Cut the top of the T-shirt, leaving ½–¾" seam allowances. The bottom of your T-shirt already will be nicely hemmed and could be a perfect opening for the case, but you will want to cut across the shirt top to eliminate as much of the neckband and collar as possible. In the end, you want the T-shirt graphic to sit on the pillow in an attractive way. Since many graphics are close to the neck of the T-shirt, be careful not to cut into the graphic. If this means that you will need to keep part of the neckband, well, so be it. Leave the sleeves on for now. (See technical notes.)

Materials

Outgrown, beloved, children's T-shirts: a 3T fits perfectly on a boudoir pillow

Extra cotton jersey: perhaps ¼ yard, which can be salvaged from another, less-beloved T-shirt

Boudoir or travel pillow, 12" × 16"

Sewing machine

Scissors

"Of course I love it. You made it and it's so special to me."

—Cedar

Sew up the sides of the shirt. Turn the T-shirt inside out, and sew the sleeve holes together along a straight line from the body. Part of the sleeve will show in the final pillow. Cut the rest of the sleeves off, leaving a ½–¾" seam allowance.

Create a matching tube of fabric the same width as the T-shirt tube to sew to the top of the T-shirt. This fabric could come from an existing T-shirt the same size as your main T-shirt and turned inside out. Depending on where you cut your original

T-shirt, this tube may need to be 3–6" with seam allowances to make the pillowcase look nice. Overall, your goal is to have the whole case be 16" in length. Sew this tube to the top of your inside-out T-shirt. If you want a slightly larger bottom on your case, sew another piece of the second T-shirt here, with the original finished bottom in place so you have a clean pillowcase opening.

To finish, sew along the top of the tube to close the case. Turn right side out.

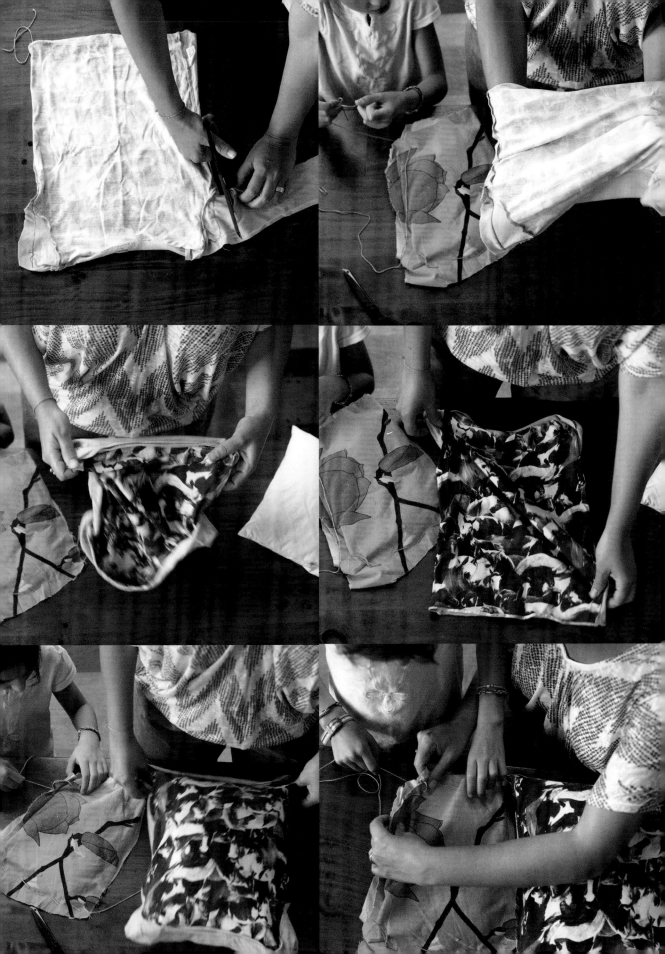

Bandana-rama

Bandanas and handkerchiefs are great building blocks
for sewing projects. I am a lazy crafter, so when I find a
project that is easy to execute—and it has prefinished
hems—I am in!

When you and your child use bandanas as the same basic building blocks, you
are on equal footing—a wonderful thing to share with a child. And both of these
projects, with their equally polished outcomes, give a real sense of satisfaction. I
helped my daughter with her stitches for the headband, but I quickly discovered
that her running stitch was straighter and smaller than mine; I went back to
machine sewing the top, letting my daughter push some of the sewing through
as the mood struck her. It's smart to work on very elementary sewing projects
with kids so that you don't get hung up on perfecting a dart or a blind hem,
which means you can allow the child to participate in the sewing process.

Handkerchief Headband Child

This project is a fun way to develop good basic sewing skills. Its polished outcome is very satisfying, and it feels like an adult project.

And yet the activity of doing fine running stitches still gets at the meditative enjoyment of crafting. Excluding the ironing, all steps are easily achievable, even to a fairly young child. The repurposing of elastic bands, I think, is actually a nice touch because it opens up those possibilities in the child's mind with other common household items.

Project Notes

The hardest element of this project is finding the handkerchiefs, since cloth ones are not readily produced. Try your local thrift store, flea markets, eBay, and yard sales. I save them up for this project. You can also use an 11" square of fabric or a fat quarter, but then you will need to finish the edges. I feel that this step takes away from the child's sense of accomplishment. See the technical notes for step-by-step illustrations.

Prepare the handkerchief by ironing it, and then fold it into the headband shape. Fold the handkerchief corner to corner so that you have a triangle. Fold the top tip of the triangle over approximately 2". Fold the bottom of the triangle up so it covers the folded-over tip and meets the other fold.

Sew along the long edges of the handkerchief with a running stitch.

Create the adjustable elastic back. Knot a few of the elastics together. Put the ends of the headband through the open loops, and secure them with a

Materials

11" square handkerchief

Thread

Needle

Safety pin

2–3 hair elastics

safety pin. Try the headband on the child's head, and adjust the number of elastics until it fits comfortably. It does not need to be tight, as this will put a lot of stress on the material.

Sew the handkerchief headband ends around the elastics using a running stitch, backstitch, or a sewing machine. Make it strong enough so it won't rip while wearing.

Bandana Top Adult

On your own, this is a very easy and satisfying project to complete in an hour. If you're working side by side with a child, you'll need an afternoon. Shared time is the essence of side-by-side crafting.

Sure, you could wait until your child is in bed (if you are blessed with one of those sleeping models of children) and crank out these tops, but where is the joy in that? If you're truly interested in efficiency, sewing bandana tops probably is not the place to start. Instead, see it as project to slow down and enjoy time with your child as you work next to each other.

Project Notes

I found these bandanas at the dollar bin at Target.

This top can be hand sewn, but I prefer sewing with a machine so it does not come apart in the wash.

A shoelace can be used instead of a ribbon, but ribbons are sweeter. See technical notes for step-by-step illustrations.

Layer the bandanas, right sides together. Place them with a corner pointing up so they make a diamond shape. Pin or baste together the left and right corners to create a straight vertical seam on each side.

Determine the width of the top, the size of the armhole opening, and the neckline by measuring the bandanas on the child. Mark on the front and back where the top corner of the bandana ought to be hemmed to create a comfortable neckline on the child. The diagonal openings at the top sides of the bandanas make perfect armholes. Adjust the shirt width as necessary.

Materials

2 bandanas

Ribbon (½ yard is plenty)

Sewing machine

Scissors

Safety pin

Sew along each side of the bandanas, leaving a ¾" seam allowance. I do not like finishing interior seams, so I tend to leave a little extra material to account for fraying.

Fold over top corners at the mark, and sew ½–¾" away from the fold to create an opening to slip ribbon through. Cut the top corners of the bandana off, leaving a ¾" seam allowance.

Attach a safety pin to the ribbon, and thread it through one bandana and then the other. Adjust the ribbon straps on the child, and tie the ribbon at one shoulder. Cut any excess.

Precious Keepsakes

By Jessica Polka

These two projects make a big deal out of small things. The necklace is made from found objects and fabric, and the tension of the draw cords is what holds the keepsake securely in place. The seaweed is created from just a few basic crochet stitches.

When Jessica showed me these projects, I knew I had to try them with my daughter, who loves all things tiny, found, and ocean themed. These projects find a way to transform a day of beach combing into something more formal and permanent. I found that the keepsake necklace needed more parental guidance to come to fruition, so the seaweed made a nice pairing since it easily could be put down and picked back up without losing my place.

Keepsake Necklace Child

Combing the beach is an archetypical parent-child activity—a great pleasure to share with a child. Some days are good for finding starfish, others for beach glass.

On a day when you find a well-worn and rounded shell, this project will help you keep that memory special. Children will need some help with ironing the fabric wrapper for the object, but the sewing and other techniques are fairly simple. The cinching together to create the final necklace is a tiny miracle.

Project Notes

See the technical notes for step-by-step illustrations.

Find a keepsake. This can be a small, round shell or a coin. It needs to be round and somewhat flat to work.

Cut a piece of fabric that is as long as the circumference of your object plus 1" to allow for ½" seam allowance on each end. (I usually just roll the object along the fabric and mark where it has made a full rotation.) The width of the fabric can be varied, depending on whether you want the back of the object exposed (for a shell) or not (a coin). If you want to cover the back of your object, cut the fabric about 1½" wider than your object. If you want the back of your object exposed, cut the fabric to 1" wider than your object.

Hem the fabric by folding each short edge in ¼" and pressing with an iron.

Lift up the long edges so that they meet in the middle. Fold over the top edge by ¼", and lay the fabric flat. The top fold line should run through the middle of the fabric (as shown in the technical notes). Press the fabric in place.

Materials

A roundish, flat, found keepsake object

Small piece of fabric

Size 10 crochet thread, or other fine string

Iron and ironing board

Cut two 24" pieces of crochet thread (I used my
arm span), and put these inside the fabric, so that
each strand runs along one edge of the fabric. It can
be helpful to tape them to a table to prevent them
from crossing.

Hand sew along the long, folded seam in the middle
of the fabric. Make sure your crochet threads are not
crossed inside the fabric.

Secure your object in the fabric by placing it in the
middle of the fabric, and scrunch up the threads
as shown.

Tie each thread to itself at the point where it emerges
from the casing you've made. Then tie both of these
sets together where they meet at the apex of the
object. At this point, you can also knot in a third
thread if you want to braid both sides.

Braid or knot the loose ends. You can either leave
them raw to be tied around the neck like a ribbon,
or you can add a button or a metal necklace binding.

Seaweed Crochet Adult

I knew Jessica's projects had to be part of this book—they have just the right combination of simplicity and fantasy. And they speak to the impetus of every project in this book—to blow your child's mind!

If you can pick up a crochet hook and create seaweed, you might really become your child's hero for a few divine minutes. I love this project because the work looks so fine and careful, and yet it can be put down at a moment's notice to help with your child's project.

Project Notes

The "sea grass" shown here was worked up in size 10 thread, but it's also fun to make in worsted weight or heavier yarn. You can also try varying the height of the stitches (double crochet or slip stitch, for instance) that you use to work back into the chains.

Descriptions of chain stitch, single stitch, and slip stitch are in the technical notes.

Simply begin with a chain. This will form the point of the leftmost stem. Chain until your work is about ½–1".

Continue to chain to create a length of stitches for the first branch.

Chain again to start a sub branch. When the sub branch is as long as you would like it (three stitches for the first small branch; see the diagram in the technical notes), single crochet back onto these new chain stitches to complete the sub branch.

Chain again to make a second sub branch, and single crochet over these stitches.

Materials

Size 10 crochet thread

U.S. 7 or 8 crochet needle

Continue to single crochet along the stem of the branch to finish it, and chain again once you are back to where you'd like the main stem to be. (A "stem" is made from chains that remain without single crochets while you start working another chain.)

Repeat as desired, and then begin single crocheting back along the stem instead of chaining again when you've finished the branch farthest from your start point.

To make new branches on the other side of the main stem, you simply chain and single crochet as before—but remember to single crochet when you reach the stem.

Continue adding length to your stem and adding branches and sub branches as you desire.

PART THREE

Family
Field Trips

These projects are great for bigger groups of kids because they involve teamwork and group problem solving.

Crafts tend to happen in the confined space of our homes and get, after a while, confining. Arguments erupt, whining begins, and that is the surefire sign it is time to get out of the house. Even in less-than-perfect weather, it's great to go out and make things.

The projects in this part are low-intensity, whimsical activities that try to foster understanding about how you can take an environment and intervene to make it magical. They are really very lovely moments of making art out of everyday life.

Spider Web

This project is pretty irresistible. It teaches weaving that is not bound to any special form. Starting the structure helps children get a conceptual grasp of the space they can use to create the spider web. With enough twine, you can start several kids altogether working in tree forks. I think it is humbling for adults and kids alike to try to re-create the delicate and intricate web of a spider.

Look at pictures of spider webs with your child.

Find a tree or bush outside with some good forks in the branches.

Tie the kitchen twine to the tree, but loosely, to not hurt it.

Build the exterior structure of the web. Begin by making a frame that creates a large, roughly circular line that attaches to several branches of the tree that exist roughly in the same planar space. Be sure to help your child, who may have difficulty visualizing how to create the outside edge of a flat web in three-dimensional space. When finished, you should have a rough circle in place.

Hand over the string to your child. This step will be hard because you will want to make the web, but let your child experiment with weaving the string within the frame you have created to make a spider web. If the children are having a hard time, make your own spider web nearby so they can see your technique. Hint: Work from the outer edges to create spokes that meet in the middle, and then tie and weave the twine through all the spokes.

Tie off and cut the twine.

"One of the best projects we've done!"

—Cedar

Materials

Kitchen twine

Scissors

Pictures of spider webs, particularly orb-structured webs

Autumn Crown

Although I call this an autumn crown, my daughter and I have done this project in the summer as well. There is always some beautiful kind of leaf that can be made into a headdress with a little imagination.

Hunting for the right materials is a huge pleasure with this project. Walking around clipping beautiful seed pods and picking up fall leaves with your kids is a fantastic treasure hunt. Smaller children will need your help stapling the leaves to the headdress. When I did this project with a group of kids, I was really surprised at the variety of approaches to the crown, each as unique as the child working on it. The simplicity and clarity in the execution of this project make it a joy to work on.

Cut a strip of brown paper 3–4" tall and wide enough to wrap around a child's head. A tube cut from a paper grocery bag is plenty long enough to do the trick.

Collect leaves and other natural materials.

Help the child staple the items to brown paper.

Fit the band around child's head, noting where the join should be. Remove from child's head, and staple together.

Materials

Stapler

Brown paper grocery bag or kraft paper

Autumn leaves and plant materials

"To make a good crown you need a mix of leaves and flowers."

—Cedar

Seed Self-Portrait

I almost can't explain how much fun this project is. Usually, a craft project's specialness is in inverse proportion to the amount of children making it. In this case, the reverse is true.

The more the merrier! Self-portraits make instantaneous sense to a child. The key to this project is setting up the proper scale. By using the body's outline as the space to fill, the drawings become dramatic and inhabit the space they occupy. I loved being able to dip in and out of helping the kids make their drawings, and then enjoy talking to other parents when not facilitating. The project was so engrossing for the kids that it was lovely just to stand back and admire their work. Be sure to bring some snacks.

Project Notes

If you don't live in a place with an outdoor garden or a feed store, you can always order seeds online (see resources). This project will attract all kinds of wildlife, so you may want to be judicious about the amount of seed and its location.

You will want to pour the colored sand into squeeze bottles the night before so that everything is ready to go.

Find a good place to create your portraits. We picked a park where we knew there would be a lot of birds.

Create the child's outline. Have your child lie on the ground (in whatever pose he or she wants!), and create an outline as well as you can, being sure to hug close to the child's body.

Let the child detail with chalk. Give your child a piece of chalk to draw details in his or her outline: face, clothes, fingers, etc.

Introduce the bird seed. Help the child fill areas of the drawing with bird seed. Use cups to carefully pour it into the outlines. Try to use the seed to fill in large areas of the drawing.

Materials

10 lbs of wild bird seed, separated by type

6–8 bags of colored sand (1 lb each)

6–8 12 oz. squeeze bottles (for the sand)

Sidewalk chalk

Paper or plastic cups

Introduce the colored sand. Put out the squeeze bottles of colored sand. Do this step last because the colored sand is very seductive, and it's meant to be used only for accent areas, and not the entire drawing.

Refill the colored sand endlessly. Children will go through a lot of colored sand. Be prepared to keep refilling the bottles.

Wait for the birds. If there isn't too much commotion, they will come.

Living Willow Teepee

By Karen Quiana

When done in a well-placed, well-watered location, this project will provide joy for years to come. A living willow teepee playhouse is a perfect spring project that combines gardening and magic.

Karen was the perfect person to teach us the power of garden magic. Seeing the structure built and then slowly grow over time is an incredible experience for adult and child alike. Using living material in this way is unusual since so much of what we craft with is "dead" matter. It is powerful to manipulate living material. Children can dip in and out of the project to help with the weaving process, while adults are on the hook to do the digging and planting. Plan a picnic lunch or a barbeque, and you will have a great day.

Project Notes

Willow rods are a specialty item that you will most likely need to order from a specialized nursery beforehand (see resources). This project is best done in early spring when nurseries have these items.

Willow varieties have various sunlight needs, so also take those needs into account when considering your teepee playhouse site. A plant nursery will be able to advise you on which types to purchase.

This project is a team effort. You will want several adults and a group of children involved.

Your willow playhouse will require annual spring pruning to keep its shape.

Pick a spot for your teepee. Find a place that gets plenty of water.

Create the circle foundation for the teepee. Measure out a 5' circle where you want the teepee. Remove all turf around the perimeter of the circle, with a spade if necessary. Doing so will allow the willows to root and grown.

Mark out the planting holes for the teepee. Measure out a doorway roughly 24" wide, and then mark 10 roughly even spaces on your circle, placing a flag marker at each. These spots are for your thickest upright rods. Between each of the 10 flags, place two more evenly spaced flags. These are for your medium thickness rods. Use the metal rod to create 1'-deep holes where you have placed your markers. The holes created by this rod provide enough depth for the willow to root well.

Materials

60 living willow rods, 6' tall:

    10 thick ¾" rods for the main uprights

    20 medium thickness ½" rods to weave diagonally through the main uprights

    30 light thickness ¼" rods for the horizontal stabilizers

Cardboard

Spade

Metal rod (to dig holes)

Flag markers

Mulch

Nearby water source

Plant the uprights. Take your thickest willow rods, and plant them in the first 10 holes, carefully backfilling any extra space. Lean them against each other toward the middle of the circle to create the teepee shape. Use twine to tie the tops together. Plant and weave the medium rods. Take your medium rods, and plant them at a slight angle to the left or right, in the direction you will weave them between the thicker willow rods. Backfill the holes carefully. Angle two adjacent medium rods to cross each other—you will weave them in opposite directions to provide more stability to the structure. Bend the medium rods so they become horizontal, and then alternate weaving over and under the uprights. Begin by weaving in the medium rods as low as possible without breaking the rods, and then weave the rods progressively higher up the teepee. Be sure to leave the door opening, weaving medium rods to create a rough archway at a comfortable height to allow people to get in and out of the teepee.

Weave in willow bands to help stabilize the structure. Take your thinnest rods, and weave them in bands at roughly the top and middle of the teepee. These rods are not planted and will not grow; rather, they help stabilize the teepee structure.

Lay down cardboard around the teepee, and then cover that with mulch in a rough circle. The cardboard will prevent other plants from growing around the teepee while the willow rods take root. It will also help keep in moisture.

Water the ground generously after planting and continue to do so every day for the first week, every other day for the next week, and then a few times a week after that as the willow rods become established.

Play! The teepee playhouse is ready to be used as a hideout and play structure as soon as you are done with the initial watering.

"I loved weaving the branches. It was fun to get in the middle."

—Cedar

Acknowledgments

I'd like to thank all the people who made this book come to fruition. Doug Lloyd, my beloved, for his fanatical encouragement and support throughout the process. Kate McKean, for taking the time to speak with me. Betsy Greer, for being awesome and making the introduction. Jennifer Urban-Brown, for her remarkable ability to clarify and focus this book, Lora Zorian, Hazel Bercholz, and the rest of the team at Roost Books, for really "getting it."

Thanks to everyone at Flat for their hard work on the design of this book; particularly to Nozlee Samadzadeh for her superlative crafting skills on Child Embroidery Drawing and Norel Hassan for her perfect illustrations. Meredith Heuer, for taking such unbelievably beautiful photographs. Contributors Diane Bromberg, Jessica Polka, and Karen Quiana, for sharing their brilliance in this book. All the children who participated in the crafting with grace and gusto: Autumn and Kailin Hartley, Alice and Margot Polen, Lily Schaeufele, Ines Seymour, Malik Shah, Edie Strianese, and August and Cleveland Wright. Not to mention their parents, who were conscripted into service. And a special thanks to Leah Adams; to Pat Quiana, for spending her Mother's Day with us; and to Joan and Peter Unterwegner, for sharing their home.

A huge thank you to the people and companies that so graciously donated materials to this book:

A Trade for a Trade, www.atradeforatrade.com

Bluestem Nursery, www.bluestem.ca

Duncraft, www.duncraft.com

cu·te·ta·pe, www.cutetape.com

Grounded, www.shopgrounded.com

Lion Brand Yarns, www.lionbrand.com

National Nonwovens, www.commonwealthfelt.com

Paradise Fibers, www.paradisefibers.com

Purl Soho, www.purlsoho.com

Slice, www.sliceproducts.com

Spoonflower, www.spoonflower.com

Finally, this book would not be possible without my daughter, Cedar. Her patience, insight, and contagious enthusiasm made every project in this book a joy. I can't thank her enough for all the light she brings into my life.

Technical Notes

Here you will find the techniques needed to create all the crafts in this book. The techniques are basic, but I always like to refresh my skills before embarking on a new project. I have also provided some additional templates to help you extend these projects and make them your own.

Giant Newspaper Snowflake
Snowflake Templates

These templates work both for the large newspaper snowflake and for smaller-scale ones folded, as in the snowflake instructions. Lightly draw these patterns onto the paper, and then cut along the lines. Remember to never cut all the way across the folded triangle.

How to Make a Pom-Pom

If you don't have a pom-pom maker, you can easily create your own. Cut two of the template shape out of cardboard. To make the pom-pom, cut a length of yarn about 10" in length and loosely lay it in an O shape between the two templates, holding the sandwiched yarn in place with your hand and letting the excess yarn hang down (see illustration). This will be the pom-pom tie. Now, start at one end of the notched circle, and start wrapping yarn from your skein around the two layers of cardboard. Continue by winding yarn around the card about 80–120 times (the fullness of the pom-pom will depend on the thickness of the fiber), ending up with a dense, notched donut shape. Tie the pom-pom tie in a loose square knot. Using scissors, start to cut the yarn around the edges of the notched circle (see illustration). Knot the square knot as tightly as possible to the center of the yarn bunch. Slip the cardboard templates out of the yarn ball, and fluff the pom-pom slightly by combing the strands with your fingers.

1

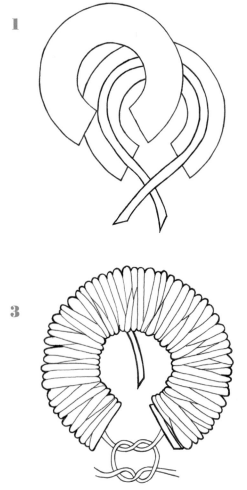

2

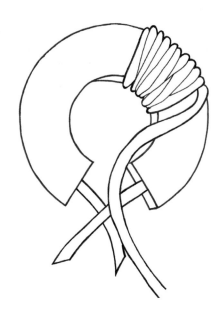

3

144

Back Stitch
Bring the thread to the front of the fabric. Insert
the needle into the fabric, one stitch to the right of
where the thread came out. Then, from the back to
the front, insert the needle into the fabric, one stitch
to the left of where the thread originally came out.
Repeat, inserting the needle so it touches the next
stitch to the right, and bringing it back up one stitch
to the left.

Indoor Succulent Gardens
Terrarium

Layer planting materials in your terrarium
for best results.

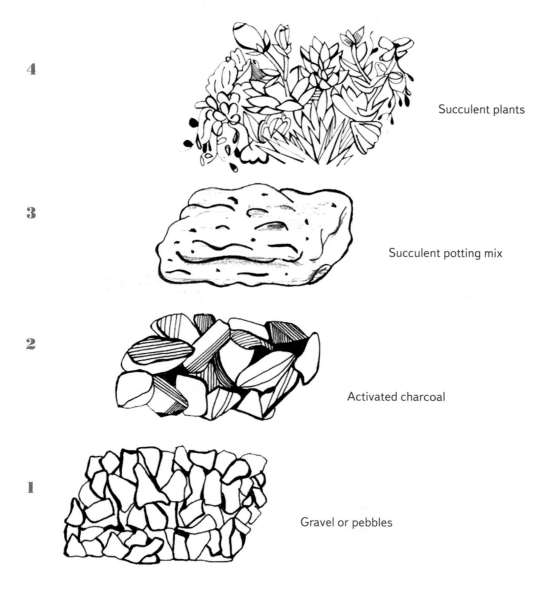

4 Succulent plants

3 Succulent potting mix

2 Activated charcoal

1 Gravel or pebbles

T-Shirt Pillow Case

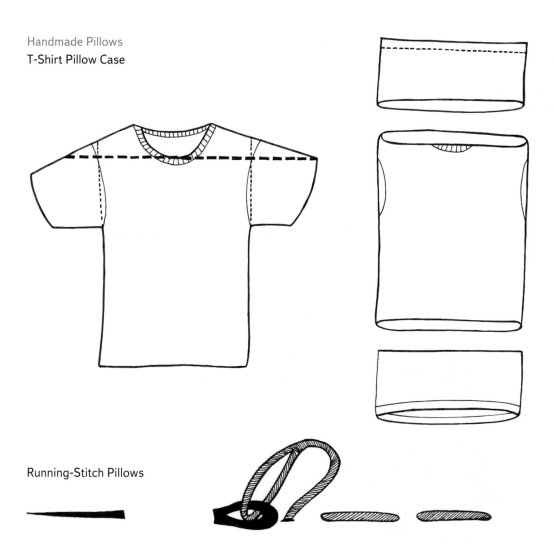

Running-Stitch Pillows

Running Stitch

Knot the thread at one end, and insert the needle into the fabric, from the back side of the fabric to the front. Reinsert the needle from the front to the back, ¼–½" away from the first stitch. Continue in this way along the seam. Once your child gets the hang of this skill, the needle can be inserted twice in one stitch, as in the illustration.

Bandana-rama
Handkerchief Headband

Bandana Top

1

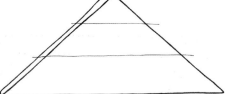

1

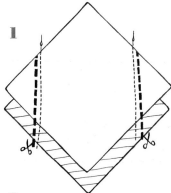

2

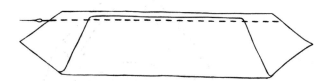

2

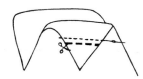

3

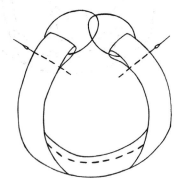

3

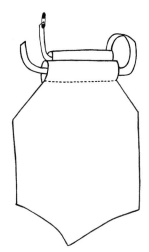

Keepsake Necklace

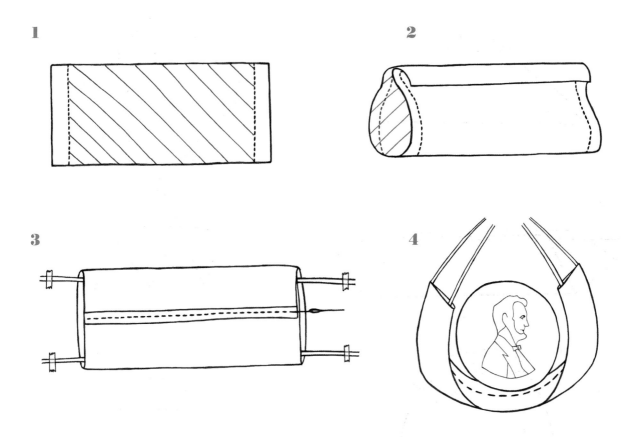

1

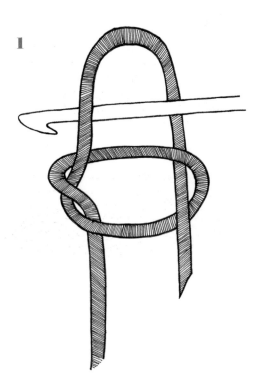

2

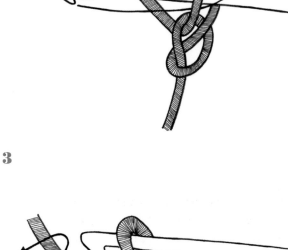

3

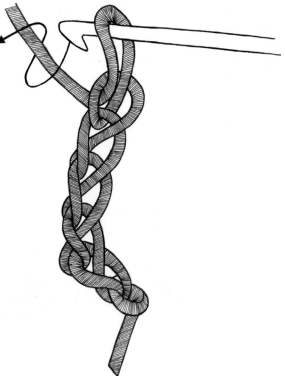

Chain Stitch

Make a slip knot, inserting the crochet hook into the knot and tightening to cast one loop on the hook. Then, hook the yarn from the skein over the hook, and draw it back through the loop, creating a new loop. Continue until you reach the desired number of stitches.

Slip Stitch

Insert the hook into the next stitch. Pass the yarn over the crochet needle, and pull it through both the stitch you just hooked into and the loop already on the hook. Repeat.

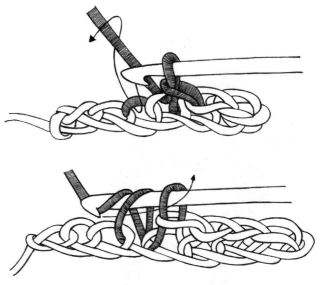

Single Crochet

Insert the hook into the next stitch. Pass the yarn over the crochet needle, and draw it through just that stitch, creating two loops on the needle. Pass the yarn over the crochet needle again, and draw it through both loops, leaving just one loop on the hook. Repeat.

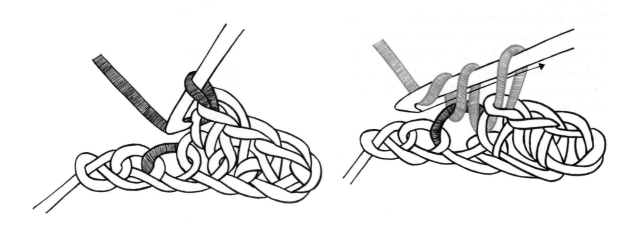

Seaweed Crochet Chart

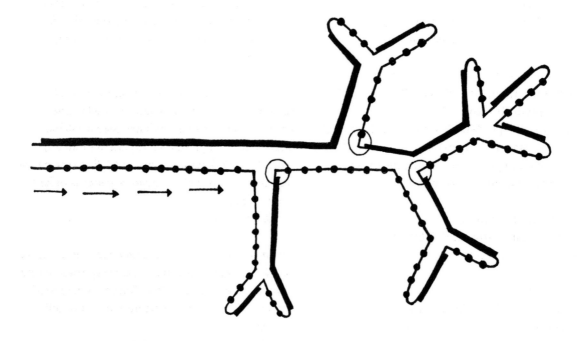

CHAIN

SINGLE CROCHET

SLIP STITCH

Resources

Pom-Pom Garland
Yarn: Lion Brand, 800-258-YARN,
www.lionbrand.com
Pom-pom maker: Purl Soho, (212) 420-8796,
www.purlsoho.com
100% wool felt: National Nonwovens, (800) 333-
3469, www.commonwealthfelt.com

Hand-Stamped Bookmarks and Stationery
Scissors and cutting tools: Slice, (408) 273-6565,
www.sliceproducts.com
Wood block stamps: A Trade for a Trade, (734) 369-
2585, www.atradeforatrade.com
Japanese masking tape: cu·te·ta·pe, cutetape@
gmail.com, www.cutetape.com

Indoor Succulent Gardens
Glass Terrariums: Grounded, (760) 230-1563,
www.shopgrounded.com

Seed Self-Portrait
Birdseed: Duncraft, (888) 879-5095,
www.duncraft.com

Living Willow Teepee
Bluestem Nursery, 250-447-6363, www.bluestem.ca

Contributors

Diane Bromberg is an artist with a history of
starting and managing innovative businesses. She
has spent the last few years putting her creative
energy toward building her own home inside of
a run-down Brooklyn building. She works at the
creative firm Flat to keep it sailing smoothly. She
is a graduate of Rhode Island School of Design.
www.futuregift.com

Jessica Polka is a biologist and designer of soft
sculpture and embroidery, and is based in San
Francisco. Her crochet work has been available
online and through shops and galleries under the
name "Wunderkammer" since 2007. She is currently
working on a book of sea creature patterns to knit
and crochet.
jpolka.blogspot.com

Karen Quiana is a landscape architect and principal
at LQ Design, an interior and landscape design firm
located in Beacon, New York. Karen has a master's
degree in Landscape Architecture from Cornell
University.
www.LQdesignhouseandgarden.com

About the Author

Tsia Carson—designer, mother, craft book author, force of nature—is a partner at the award-winning New York City–based design firm Flat (www.flat.com) and is the founder of SuperNaturale (www.supernaturale.com), an alternative crafts site. Her first book, *Craftivity*, was selected as Amazon's Best Books of 2006: Top 10 Editors' Picks: Home & Garden. She has been a visiting critic in the graduate design programs at Yale, Maryland Institute College of Art, and Rhode Island School of Design and frequently tests out new projects with her daughter, Cedar, in both the craft and digital realms.

About the Photographer

An award-winning, self-trained photographer, Meredith Heuer has shot for *Fortune*, *Gourmet*, and *Travel & Leisure*. She approaches all her subject matter—living or inanimate—as an opportunity to explore intimacy and grace. She is currently working on the Beacon Portrait in Beacon, New York, where she resides with her husband, two sons, and three meandering chickens. You can see her work at www.meredithheuer.com